The Musicians' Joke Book

music n. A complex organization of sounds that is set down by a composer, incorrectly interpreted by a conductor, who is ignored by musicians, the result of which is disregarded by an audience and slated by critics.

Jim Green

OMNIBUS PRESS
part of The Music Sales Group

London / New York / Paris / Sydney / Copenhagen / Berlin / Madrid / Tokyo

Introduction by Jim Green

It's not hard to see why musicians have a dark sense of humour. As members of "the second oldest profession" we're outsiders. Nobody in their right mind travels as much as we do, often putting up with terrible lodgings, bad food and no sleep. So it's not surprising we're a band apart (so to speak), outcasts who seek only our own company, rubbing two jokes together for warmth and trying to feel superior by sneering at one another's abilities and personalities. And I'm not just talking about rock music either. All musicians seem attracted to black humour.

Many years ago, after I was thrown out of one of London's most famous music colleges (for welding the slides of an entire trombone section into fixed positions), I tried to earn some money playing in the orchestra of a touring musical called Pop! From the start I never really thought that the story of the Hindenberg disaster was really suited to the format of the stage musical, but such things were in fashion at the time and Pop! was just the latest in a string of shows that included Lionel Bart's Twang! (a musical version of Robin Hood) and Splash! (the story of the Titanic set to music). Pop! played to near-empty houses all over the United Kingdom until the night a serious electrical fault caused a much bigger explosion than the one normally created by sound effects and flashing stage lights. The small audience went wild as real sparks and flashes erupted, the scenery caught fire and several actors received near-fatal electric shocks. The next night people queued around the block to get in, but unfortunately this and all future performances had to be cancelled as many of the company were now in intensive care. As a result, my trombone introduction to 'Up, Up and Away' was obviously surplus to requirements and that was that.

Such experiences can be discouraging and so I decided to leave serious music altogether and start my own rock band called The Giants, in which I played lead guitar and sang. This is where I first heard all those jokes about guitarists, singers, bass players and drummers.

For my fellow band members, these jokes were only offensive when they targeted their particular instrument. As a multi-instrumentalist – I play drums, guitar, bass, piano, trombone, violin, mandolin, clarinet, trumpet, oboe and French horn – I found myself on the receiving end of almost every gag. I can tell you, without a sense of humour I wouldn't have lasted long! I had to retaliate and so my reputation as a practical joker began in earnest and on more than one occasion led to the threat of prosecution. Once I filled a set of bagpipes with lemon juice, and if the aggrieved owner hadn't made the mistake of telling the magistrate that the whole incident had "...left a bitter taste in his mouth" – causing much unintentional hilarity in the courtroom – things might have gone badly for me. Things did go badly for me when the demon drink took hold in the 1980s and I was forced to relocate to Holland for a time to recover and to plan my return to show business. The rest is now history. But I still remember the darkest days when only a joke, a shaggy dog story or an outrageous prank could relieve the pain and boredom of the working musician's life. Now this recollected treasury of musical humour has been brought together in one volume and can be shared by everyone. Enjoy!

Jim Green

Published by

Omnibus Press

14-15 Berners Street, London W1T 3LJ, UK.

Exclusive Distributors:

Music Sales Limited

Distribution Centre, Newmarket Road,

Bury St. Edmunds, Suffolk IP33 3YB, UK.

Music Sales Corporation

257 Park Avenue South, New York, NY10010,

United States of America.

Music Sales Pty Limited

20 Resolution Drive, Caringbah, NSW 2229, Australia.

Design & art direction by Michael Bell Design.

Illustrated by Andy Hammond.

Printed in the EU.

Flutes & Piccolos

What is the range of a piccolo?

Q: What is the range of a piccolo?
A: About twenty yards on a good day.

Q: Why do you hardly ever see a flautist take a breath?
A: Because they already have a vast supply of air in their heads.

Q: What's the difference between a flautist and a seamstress?
A: A seamstress tucks up frills.

Q: How many flautists does it take to change a light bulb?
A: Five. One to change the bulb, one to pull the ladder out from under her and three to bitch about how much better they would have done it.

Q: What do you call a good flute section?
A: Impossible.

....

"Hell is full of musical amateurs"
George Bernard Shaw Dramatist/Critic

....

Q: How many flautists does it take to change a light bulb?
A: Just one, but she'll have to twist it back and forth for an hour to make sure she gets it just right.

....

"The only good thing to come out of religion was the music"
George Carlin Comedian

....

Q: How can you tell if a plane is full of flute players?
A: When the engines stop, the whining continues.

Q: How many flautists does it take to change a light bulb?
A: Only one, but she'll break 10 bulbs before she realizes you can't just push them in.

> ## "I got to try the bagpipes.
> It was like trying to blow an octopus"
>
> **James Galway** Flautist

Q: How do you get two piccolo players to play in unison?
A: Shoot one.

Q: What is the definition of perfect pitch in a piccolo?
A: When you throw it in the toilet and it doesn't hit the rim.

Q: How many flautists does it take to change a light bulb?
A: Just one. She simply holds it up and the world revolves around her.

> ## "The flute is not an instrument that has a good moral effect – it is too exciting"
>
> **Aristotle** Philosopher

Q: Why do loud, obnoxious whistles exist at some factories?
A: To give us some sort of appreciation for flutes.

Q: What's the definition of a minor second?
A: Two flautists playing in unison.

Oboes

Why play the oboe?

Q: Why play the oboe?
A: The case is a good weapon in emergencies.

14

Oboes

There was a young lady named Cager
Who, as a result of a wager,
Consented to fart
The whole oboe part
  Of Mozart's Quartet in F major.

Q: Why did the chicken cross the road?
A: To get away from the oboe recital.

> "All first oboists are gangsters. They are tough, irascible, double-reed roosters, feared by colleagues and conductors"

Harry Ellis Dickson Writer/Raconteur/Conductor

Q: What is a burning oboe good for?
A: Setting fire to a bassoon.

Q: What is the definition of a semitone?
A: Two oboes playing in unison.

> "I would advise you to keep your overheads down... avoid a major drug habit... play every day... and take it in front of other people... they need to hear it and you need them to hear it"

James Taylor Musician

Q: What's the difference between an oboist and a psychiatric ward patient?
A: Nothing. The oboist just hasn't been caught yet.

Q: What's the difference between an oboe playing in tune and Star Trek?
A: Star Trek could actually happen one day.

Q: When should an oboist change their reed?
A: Whenever a difficult section comes up in the score.

"An oboe is an ill wind that nobody blows good"

Bennet Cerf Author/Humorist

Q: How do you get an oboist to play an A flat?
A: You take the batteries out of his electronic tuning device and ask him to play an A.

"Only become a musician if there is absolutely no other way you can make a living"

Kirke Mechem Composer

Oboes

A community orchestra was plagued by attendance problems. Several musicians were absent at each rehearsal. As a matter of fact, every player in the orchestra had missed several rehearsals, except for one very faithful oboe player.

Finally, as the dress rehearsal drew to a close, the conductor took a moment to thank the oboist for her faithful attendance. She humbly responded "It's the least I could do, since I won't be at the performance."

Clarinets

What is the difference
between a clarinet and an onion?

Q: What is the difference between a clarinet and an onion?

A: No one cries when you chop a clarinet into little pieces.

Q: Why was the clarinettist staring at the orange juice bottle?

A: Because the label said concentrate.

Q: How many clarinettists does it take to change a light bulb?

A: One, but he needs a whole suitcase of bulbs until he finds the right one.

Q: In hospital, what's the difference between the use of the clarinet and the saxophone?

A: The saxophone is used to lull crying babies to sleep and the clarinet to wake coma patients.

clarionet [sic] n. An instrument of torture operated by a person with cotton in his ears. There are two instruments that are worse than a clarionet — two clarionets.

Ambrose Bierce The Devil's Dictionary, 1911

Q: What's the purpose of the bell on a bass clarinet?

A: To store the ashes from the rest of the instrument.

Q: What's the difference between a clarinet solo and scraping your nails down the blackboard?

A: Vibrato.

Q: What's the definition of a real nerd?

A: Someone who owns his own alto clarinet.

Q: Is there any difference between the sound of a clarinet and that of a cat in heat?

A: Of course there is, but only if the cat's in good health.

Q: Why do clarinettists place their cases on the dashboard?

A: So they can park in handicapped spaces.

A bass clarinettist missed the point where he
was supposed to come in to play.
The conductor shouted, "Hey, bass clarinet! Your turn!"
The musician turned to his instrument and said,
"Hey you, I think he's talking to you!"

Q: Why don't they make mutes for clarinets?
A: It would take a lot more than a mute to make a
clarinet sound good.

....

"He has Van Gogh's ear for music"
Orson Welles Film Actor/Director/Writer

....

Q: How do you get a clarinettist out of a tree?
A: Cut the noose.

Q: Why aren't there very many alto clarinet jokes?
A: Most people have better things to do with their time.

....

"Without music, life would be an error"
Friedrich Nietzsche Philosopher/Writer

....

**Q: Why do clarinettists stand for long periods
outside people's houses?**
A: They can't find the key and they don't know where
   to come in.

Q: How do you stop an oboe being stolen?
A: Put it in a clarinet case.

Bassoons

What are bassoons good for?

Q: What are bassoons good for?

A: Kindling an accordion fire.

Q: Which is better, a bassoon or an oboe?

A: A bassoon – it makes more tooth picks.

Q: What is the bassoon's nickname?

A: The farting bedpost.

....

"It [the bassoon] is a bass instrument without proper bass strength, oddly weak in sound, bleating burlesque"

Thomas Mann Novelist/Critic

....

"The bassoon in the orchestra plays the same role as Gorgonzola among cheeses – a figure of fun. Actually, the bassoon can be the most romantic and passionate of instruments and Gorgonzola can be the finest of cheeses, but they must both be treated properly"

Cecil Gray Music Critic/Composer

....

Q: How many bassoonists does it take to change a light bulb?

A: Only one, but they'll insist on going through about five bulbs before they find one that suits the particular room and situation.

Bassoons

Saxophones

What's the difference
between a lawnmower and a tenor sax?

Q: What's the difference between a lawnmower and a tenor sax?
A: You can tune a lawnmower.

Q: ...And another difference between a lawnmower and a tenor sax?
A: Lawnmowers sound better in small ensembles.

Q: ...And the third difference between a lawnmower and a tenor sax?
A: The neighbours would be upset if you borrowed their lawnmower and didn't return it.

....

"The saxophone is the embodied spirit of beer"

Arnold Bennett English Writer

....

One day, a saxophone player was driving down the freeway, when he hit two flute players who were crossing the road. One went through the windshield and the other flew about thirty feet down the road. When the policeman interviewed the driver, he said, "Oh, so you're a sax player too, huh? Well, I think I know how we can get these two flautists. I can arrest one for breaking and entering and the other for leaving the scene of the crime."

Q: Why did the soprano bed four different saxophone players from the same band in a single night?
A: She was a sax maniac.

Q: What is black and brown and looks good on a saxophonist?
A: A Doberman.

Q: If you were lost in the desert, who would you ask for directions, an in-tune tenor sax player, an out-of-tune tenor sax player, or Santa Claus?
A: The out-of-tune tenor sax player – the other two would be hallucinations.

Q: What do you call a saxophonist who plays mostly hemidemisemiquavers?
A: A ballad specialist.

Q: What is the difference between a saxophone and a chainsaw?
A: It's all in the grip.

Q: How many alto sax players does it take to change a light bulb?
A: Five. One to do it, and four to comment on how John Coltrane would have done it.

Q: What's the difference between the creationist theory of the origin of life and a tenor sax?
A: The theory doesn't have as many leaks.

Q: What are the differences between a baritone sax and a chain saw?
A: Vibrato and the exhaust.

....

"Music makes one feel so romantic –
at least it always gets on one's nerves –
which is the same thing nowadays"
Oscar Wilde Irish Playwright

....

Saxophones

The reason why so many weird noises come out of the business end of saxophones is that Adolph Sax never issued any instructions on how to play them. Contrary to popular belief, saxophones are percussion instruments and are meant to be beaten with hammers...large hammers.

Q: Why did censors ban the airing of a documentary programme on BBC television that purported to introduce young people to the worlds of jazz and classical music?
A: Too much sax and violins.

French horns

Why is the French horn a
divine instrument?

Q: Why is the French horn a divine instrument?
A: Because a man blows in it, but only God knows what comes out of it.

French horns

Q: How do you get a French horn to sound like a trombone?
A: Stick your hand in the bell and mess up all the notes.

Q: How do you know that a horn player is about to drop in on you?
A: The doorbell has missed the tune.

Q: How many horn players does it take to change a light bulb?

A: Just one, but he'll spend two hours checking the bulb for alignment and leaks.

Q: What is the difference between a French horn section and a '57 Chevy?

A: You can tune a '57 Chevy.

Q: What do you get when you cross a horn player and a goalpost?

A: A goalpost that can't march.

....

"Just because you can record, doesn't mean you should"

Christopher Knab

Music Business Consultant

....

Q: What is the difference between a squirrel and a horn player in the back of a taxi?

A: The squirrel is probably going to a gig.

Q: Which is the ideal place to practise a French horn?...

a. In a nature reserve;

b. Five fathoms under the surface of the Pacific Ocean;

c. In a deserted coal mine;

d. None of the above.

A: The correct answer is (d). A horn player never, never practises – the risk of learning to play would be too great.

> "After silence, that which comes nearest to expressing the inexpressible is music"

Aldous Huxley English Author

Q: How do horn players traditionally greet each other?
A: "Hi. I did that piece in junior high."

> "The horn, the horn, the lusty horn
> Is not a thing to laugh to scorn"

William Shakespeare Playwright, from As You Like It

French horns

There once was a woman who had gone a long time without so much as a hope of having a relationship. When she finally picked up a handsome-looking guy and went out with him, her friends were naturally curious as to how it went. "What's he like?" asked a friend the day after the big event. "Oh, he's fine, I guess. He's a musician, you know," she replied. "Did he have class?" enquired the friend. The friend's ears pricked up as the woman said, "Well, most of the time, yes, but I don't think I'll be going out with him again." "Oh? Why not?" asked the friend. "Well, he plays the French horn, so I guess it's just a habit, but every time we kiss, he sticks his fist in my rear!"

Q: How do you get your viola section to sound like the horn section?
A: Ask them to miss every other note.

Trumpets

Why can't a gorilla play the trumpet?

Q: Why can't a gorilla play the trumpet?

A: He'd be too sensitive.

Q: How do you improve the aerodynamics of a trumpeter's car?

A: Take the Domino's Pizza sign off the roof.

....

"Don't play what's there, play what's not there"

Miles Davis American Jazz Trumpeter/Composer

....

"I'll play it first and tell you what it is later"

Miles Davis American Jazz Trumpeter/Composer

....

Trumpets

In an emergency, a jazz trumpeter was hired to do some solos with a symphony orchestra. Everything went fine through the first movement, when she had some really hair-raising solos, but in the second movement she started improvising madly when she wasn't supposed to play at all.

After the concert, the conductor came round looking for an explanation. She said, "I looked in the score and it said 'tacet' – so I took it!"

Q: What did little Johnny's mother tell him when he said, "I want to be a trumpet player when I grow up"?

A: "But Johnny, you can't do both."

Q: What are trumpets made out of?

A: Leftover saxophone parts.

**Q: How many trumpeters does it take to change
a light bulb?**
A: Five. One to hold it in place and four to drink beer
until the room spins.

Q: What do trumpet players use for birth control?
A: Their personalities.

Q: What did the brass player perform for free?
A: The *Trumpet Voluntary*.

Trumpets

> "Brass bands are all very well
> in their place—outdoors and several
> miles away"

Sir Thomas Beecham Conductor

senza sordino *adj.* A term used to remind a trumpeter that he forgot to put his mute on a few bars back.

Q: How do you know when a trumpet player is at your door?

A: The door shrieks.

Trombones

What was written on
the trombonist's tombstone?

Q: What was written on the trombonist's tombstone?

A: 'Old trombonists never die, they just slide away.'

Q: **What did the trombone player do when he won the lottery?**

A: Silly – trombone players can't afford lottery tickets.

Q: **What is another term for a trombone?**

A: A wind-driven, manually-operated pitch approximator.

....

"Never look at the trombones, it only encourages them"

Richard Strauss German Composer

....

Q: **What's the least used sentence in the English language?**

A: "Look at that trombone player's Rolls Royce!"

Q: **What's the difference between a boxer and a trombone player?**

A: Boxers are supposed to hurt people with their talent.

Q: **How many trombonists does it take to change a light bulb?**

A: Only one, but he'll spend half an hour trying to figure out what position it needs to be in.

Q: **How can you tell that a kid in a playground is a trombonist's kid?**

A: He can't swing and he complains about the slide.

Q: What is the difference between a trombone and a trumpet?

A: A trombone will bend before it breaks.

Q: What do you call a trombone player in the street?

A: A beggar.

Q: How do you know when a trombone player is at your door?

A: The doorbell drags.

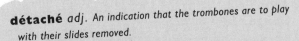

détaché adj. An indication that the trombones are to play with their slides removed.

Q: What kind of calendar does a trombonist use for his gigs?
A: A Year-at-a-Glance.

Q: How do you save a trombonist from drowning?
A: Take your foot off his head.

Q: What's the difference between a bass trombone and a chain saw?
A: Vibrato.

Q: ...And what's another difference between a bass trombone and a chain saw?
A: It's easier to improvise on a chainsaw.

Q: What do you call a trombonist with a pager?
A: The ultimate optimist.

....

"Music is a beautiful opiate, if you don't take it too seriously"

Henry Miller American Novelist

....

Q: What is the dynamic range of a bass trombone?
A: On or off.

Q: What should you do if you run over a trombonist?
A: Back up to double check that you got him.

Q: How many trombonists does it take to change a light bulb?
A: Five. One to change it, and four to make ludicrous innuendoes.

Tubas

What do you call 500 tuba players buried up to their necks in sand?

Q: What do you call 500 tuba players buried up to their necks in sand?

A: Insufficient sand.

Q: What is the range of a tuba?
A: Twenty yards if you've got a good arm.

"I hate music, especially when it's played"

Jimmy Durante Comedian

Q: There are two tuba players sitting in a car. Who's driving?
A: A policeman.

Q: What do you call 50 tuba players at the bottom of the sea?
A: A good start.

....

"Music is spiritual.
The music business is not"
Van Morrison Musician

....

"People never write pretty melodies
for tubas. It just isn't done"
George Kleinsinger Composer of Tubby The Tuba

....

Tuba Player: Did you hear my last recital?
Friend: I hope so.

Q: How do you fix a broken tuba?
A: With a tuba glue.

Q: How do you make a million playing the tuba?
A: You start with two million.

Two tuba players walked past a bar...well, it could happen!

crescendo n. *An indication to the tuba player that they have been playing too loudly.*

An orchestra was rehearsing a piece in which the tuba has a solo after 84 bars rest. At the point where the tuba should have started the solo, nothing happened. So the conductor stopped and asked the tuba player why he wasn't playing. "I have 84 bars rest," came the reply. "But we are past those 84 bars already," the conductor reasoned. The tuba player asked, "How should I know that?" The conductor said, "You can count, can't you?", to which the indignant tuba player replied, "Do you call that rest?"

bar line *n.* *A gathering of people, usually among which will be found a tuba player or two.*

Tubas

Q: How do you put a twinkle in a tuba player's eye?
A: Shine a flashlight in his ear.

....

"The tuba is certainly the most intestinal of instruments, the very lower bowel of music"

Peter De Vries Editor/Novelist

....

Q: How many professional tuba players does it take to change a light bulb?
A: None. Professional tuba players can't afford new light bulbs.

Q: What's the definition of an optimist?
A: A tuba player with a mortgage.

Violins

How do you tell the difference between a violinist and a dog?

Q: How do you tell the difference between a violinist and a dog?

A: The dog knows when to stop scratching.

Q: **Why are violins smaller than violas?**
A: They aren't – it's the violinists' heads that are larger.

Q: **Why do most people take an instant dislike to violinists?**
A: It saves time.

Q: What do a violin and a lawsuit have in common?
A: Everyone is happy when the case is closed.

"Music with dinner is an insult both to the cook and violinist"

G K Chesterton English Author/Poet/Columnist

Q: What's the difference between a violin and a fiddle?
A: A fiddle is fun to listen to.

Q: ...And another difference between a violin and a fiddle?
A: No one minds if you spill beer on a fiddle.

"Haven't I seen you somewhere before?" the judge asked the accused. "Yes you have, your honour," was the hopeful reply, "I taught your son violin last winter." "Yes, right," the judge remembered..."Twenty years!"

fiddle n. An instrument to tickle human ears by friction of a horse's tail on the entrails of a cat.
Ambrose Bierce The Devil's Dictionary, 1911

Q: Why did the Second Violinist attack the First Oboist?
A: Because he'd turned down one of his tuning pegs and wouldn't tell him which one.

Q: How can you tell if a violin is out of tune?
A: The bow is moving.

Q: What do you call a horse-drawn vehicle which delivers Italian take-aways?
A: A Pizza-carto.

....

> "Musicians own music because
> music owns them. Leave your mind
> alone and see what happens"
>
> **Virgil Thomson** American Composer

....

When we say a violinist's fingers are like lightning, what we mean is that they rarely hit the same spot twice.

Q: Why should you never try to drive in a nail with a violin?
A: You might bend the nail.

string quartet n. A group comprising a good violinist, a bad violinist, an ex-violinist and someone who hates violins and sits around complaining about composers.

> "I know only two tunes.
> One of them is 'Yankee Doodle'
> and the other isn't"
>
> **Ulysses S Grant** US President

....

String players' motto:
"It's better to be sharp than out of tune."

Q: Why do violinists get antsy when they see the Kama Sutra?

A: All those positions.

....

> "Music is a higher revelation
> than all wisdom and philosophy"
>
> **Ludwig van Beethoven** Composer

....

Q: Why don't viola players suffer from piles?

A: Because all the assholes are in the first violin section.

> ## "Had I learned to fiddle,
> I should have done nothing else"
> **Dr Samuel Johnson** English Writer

Q: When is a bow dangerous?
A: When it's a bow and arrow.

> ## "I always said God was against art
> and I still believe it"
> **Edward Elgar** English Composer

Q: What is the range of a violin?
A: As far as you can kick it.

Q: What kind of peg can't you use to hang your clothes to dry?
A: A tuning peg.

> ## "Difficult do you call it, sir?
> I wish it were impossible"
> **Dr Samuel Johnson** English Writer
> Remarking on a violinist's playing

Q: Why are viola jokes so short?
A: So violinists can understand them.

Violas

What happens when a violist dies?

Q: What happens when a violist dies?

A: They move him back a desk.

Violas

Q: Why are violists often seen congregating outside the stage door?

A: Because no one knows when to come in.

Q: What's the difference between a viola and a vacuum cleaner?

A: The vacuum has a better tone.

Q: How do you make a violin sound like a viola?
A: Sit in the back and don't play.

Q: ...And another way to make a violin sound like a viola?
A: Play in the low register with a lot of wrong notes.

Q: What is the difference between the first and last desk of a viola section?
A: Half a bar.

Q: ...And another difference between the first and last desk of a viola section?
A: A semitone.

Q: What is the difference between a violin and a viola?
A: A viola burns longer.

Q: ...And why does a viola burn longer than a violin?
A: It is usually still in the case.

Q: Why shouldn't violists take up mountaineering?
A: Because if they get lost, it takes ages before anyone notices that they're missing.

Q: What is the difference between a chainsaw and a viola?
A: If you absolutely had to, you could use a chainsaw in a string quartet.

A violist and a cellist were standing on a sinking ship. "Help!" cried the cellist, "I can't swim!"
"Don't worry," said the violist, "just fake it."

Q: How do you keep a violin from getting stolen?
A: Put it in a viola case.

Q: Why do violists have pea-sized brains?
A: Because alcohol has swelled them.

Q: What's the difference between a viola and a lawn mower?
A: The lawn mower vibrates.

Q: Why isn't a viola like a lawn mower?
A: Nobody minds if you borrow their viola.

clef n. Something to jump from before the viola solo.

Violas

A cellist and three violists walked into a restaurant.
Presently a waiter came over to serve them.
"Good evening sir," he said to the cellist, "and what would you like to eat tonight?"
"I'd like a rump steak, medium rare," replied the cellist.
"Would you like anything with that?"
"What do you have?"
"Salad?" suggested the waiter.
"No thank you," said the cellist.
"Potatoes?"
"Er, no."
"Vegetables?"
"Oh, they'll have what I'm having."

Q: What's the difference between a dead skunk in the road and a crushed viola in the road?
A: You'll see skid marks before the skunk.

Q: What is the difference between a viola and a trampoline?
A: You take off your shoes before you jump on the trampoline.

Q: ...And another difference between a viola and a trampoline?
A: About three decibels.

Q: Why don't violists play hide and seek?
A: Because no one will look for them.

Q: How many violists does it take to screw in a light bulb?

A: None. They're not small enough to fit.

A violist came home and found his house burned to the ground. When he asked what happened, the police told him, "Well, apparently the conductor came to your house, and..." The violist's eyes lit up and he interrupted excitedly, "The conductor...came to my house?"

cluster chord n. Sound produced when a viola section plays an open C string.

Q: What is the most frequent request a viola player receives?

A: A Big Mac and fries please.

A viola player decided that he'd had enough of being a viola player, of being unappreciated and the butt of all those silly jokes. So he resolved to change instruments. He went into a shop and said, "I want to buy a violin." The man behind the counter looked at him for a moment and then said, "You must be a viola player." The viola player was astonished and said, "Well...yes...I am – but how on earth did you know?" "Well sir," came the reply, "this is a fish-and-chip shop."

Q: How do you get a viola section to play *spiccato*?

A: Write a semibreve with 'solo' above it.

Q: What's the most popular recording of William Walton's Viola Concerto?

A: Music Minus One.

A violinist noticed that at the end of each rehearsal break, one of the violists would look at the inside flap of his jacket before he sat down to resume playing. This continued for several years and the violinist became quite curious about it. One day, during hot weather, the violist took off his jacket and went off on a break. The violinist waited until everyone was off the platform, looked around, and sneaked over to the jacket. He pulled back the flap and saw a little note pinned on the inside. It read: viola left hand, bow right.

Q: If you're lost in the desert, what do you aim for – a good viola player, a bad viola player or an oasis?
A: The bad viola player. The other two are only figments of your imagination.

....

"Drugs have nothing to do with the creation of music. In fact, they are dumb and self-indulgent. Kind of like sucking your thumb!"
Courtney Love Singer

....

A viola player went to a piano recital. After the performance he went up to the pianist and said, "You know, I particularly liked that piece you played last – the one that started with a long trill." The pianist said, "Huh? I didn't play any pieces that started with trills." The viola player said, "You know," and proceeded to hum the opening bars of Beethoven's Für Elise.

Q: What do you call a person who plays the viola?
A: A violator.

"Pop music is the classical music of now"

Paul McCartney Pop Singer/Songwriter/
Instrumentalist/Composer/Member of The Beatles

"Ambition is a dream with a V8 engine"

Elvis Presley Rock'n'Roll Singer/Guitarist/Actor

Violas

There was a boy in kindergarten who played the viola. One day, he came home and said, "Mummy, today we practiced counting! I got all the way up to 10, but most of the kids messed up around 6 or 7!" His mum said, "Good, that's because you're a violist." The next day he came home and said, "Mummy, today we practiced the alphabet! I got all the way to the end, but most of the kids got messed up around s or t!" and his mum replied, "Good, that's because you're a violist."
The next day, he came home and said "Mummy, guess what – they measured us today and I'm the tallest person in the whole class! Is that because I'm a violist, too?" and his mum said, "No dear – that's because you're 25 years old."

Q: How do you get a violist to play a passage
pianissimo tremolando?
A: Write 'solo' above it.

Cellos

How do you get a cello to sound beautiful?

Q: How do you get a cello to sound beautiful?
A: Sell it and buy a violin.

Q: Why shouldn't you drive off a cliff in a minivan with three cellos in it?
A: You could fit in at least one more.

Q: Why is playing the cello like peeing in your pants?
A: They both give you a nice warm feeling without making any sound.

Q: A conductor and a cellist are standing in the middle of the road. Which one do you run over first, and why?
A: The conductor – business before pleasure.

Cellos

....

"Madam, you have between your legs an instrument capable of giving pleasure to thousands, and all you can do is scratch it!"

Sir Thomas Beecham English Conductor

....

Q: Why can't you hear a cello on a digital recording?
A: Recording technology has reached such an advanced level of development that all extraneous noise is eliminated.

Q: Did you hear about the cellist who bragged that he could play demisemiquavers?
A: The rest of the orchestra didn't believe him, so he proved it by playing one.

Q: What's the difference between a cello and a coffin?
A: The coffin has the dead person on the inside.

glissando n. *A technique adopted by cellists for difficult runs.*

Q: How do you get a cellist to play fortissimo?
A: You write *pp espressivo*.

....

"Ah music! What a beautiful art!
But what a wretched profession!"
Georges Bizet French Composer

....

Q: Why is a cello solo like a bomb?
A: By the time you hear it, it's too late to do anything about it.

half step n. *The pace used by a cellist when carrying his instrument.*

Q: Did you hear about the cellist who went to a rave?
A: He asked for an 'A'.

....

"Extraordinary how potent
cheap music is"
Noel Coward English Composer/Writer/Entertainer

....

Q: How do you know when a cellist has tightened up their bow too much?
A: It looks like Robin Hood's bow.

Cellos

Double Basses

How many bass players does it take to change a light bulb?

Q: How many bass players does it take to change a light bulb?

A: None. They can't get up that high.

A double bass player arrived a few minutes late for the first rehearsal of the local choral society's annual performance of Handel's Messiah. He picked up his instrument and bow and turned his attention to the conductor. The conductor asked, "Would you like a moment to tune?" The bass player replied with some surprise, "Why? Isn't it in the same key as last year?"

Q: How do you make a double bass sound in tune?

A: Chop it up and make it into a xylophone.

virtuoso n. A musician with very high morals (I know one).

Tunnel Vision

Two bass players had been hired for a staging of Carmen. After a few weeks, they agreed that each of them should take a day off to watch the performance from outside. Thus, the first one took his free afternoon watching the opera. Upon his return to the orchestra, the other one asked him how it was. "Great," the first one replied, "You know, at that bit where the music goes 'BOM Bom Bom Bom', there are a bunch of guys singing a super song."

Q: How many bass players does it take to change a light bulb?

A: None. The piano player can do that with his left hand.

"The bouncer was outside
throwing them in"

Ronnie Scott London Jazz Nightclub Owner/
Saxophonist/Bandleader
About a poorly-attended performance

Following the success of a violin book entitled A Tune In A Day and one for cellists called A Tune In A Month, a publisher decided to produce one for bass players entitled A Tune.

Did you hear about the bassist who was so out of tune his section noticed?!?!

....

"Of all noises I think music the least disagreeable"

Dr Samuel Johnson English Writer

....

Double Basses

A man goes on vacation to a tropical island. As soon as he gets off the plane, he hears drums. He goes to the beach...he hears the drums, he eats lunch... he hears drums, he goes to a luau...he hears drums. He tries to go to sleep, but he still hears drums. This goes on for several nights and gets to the point where he can't sleep at night for the noise. Finally, he goes down to the hotel reception. When he gets there, he asks the manager, "Hey! What's with these drums – don't they ever stop? I can't get any sleep."
The manager says, "No! Drums must never stop. It's very bad if drums stop." "Why?"
"When drums stop...bass solo begins."

Q: How many bass players does it take to change a light bulb?
   A: I V I V I V...

Harps

Why are harps like elderly parents?

Q: Why are harps like elderly parents?
A: Both are unforgiving and hard to get in and out of cars.

quarter tone n. *Sound produced by a harpist when tuning unison strings.*

Q: How long does a harp stay in tune?
A: About 20 minutes, or until someone opens a door.

....

"Hang the harpers wherever found"
Queen Elizabeth I Proclamation of 1603

....

Guitars

How do you get a
guitar player to play softer?

Q: How do you get a guitar player to play softer?

A: Give him a sheet of music.

> "Rock has the ability to embarrass
> you several years later. It takes itself
> seriously, whereas Pop never pretends
> to have any depth"

Jonathan Ross English Television Presenter

counterpoint *n. The sound produced when two guitarists play in unison.*

A friend of mine was doing one of these working men's clubs up north. I asked him, "Are they any better these days?" He said, "No, still as bad. Last week I was doing this club with a trio and we were due on at nine. At about ten-to-nine the bass player and the drummer went to set their gear up and I sat in the dressing room tuning up my guitar. And the club chairman comes in and says 'Hey, they're waiting for you, what are you doing?' I said 'I'm tuning my guitar'. He said 'Come on, you've known about this bloody show for months...'"

Q: How many guitarists does it take to change a light bulb?

A: Five. One to change the bulb and four to comment on how Hendrix would have done it.

Q: What's the best thing to play on a guitar?

A: Solitaire.

Q: Why bury guitar players 6 feet under?
A: Because deep down they're all very nice people.

Did you hear about the guitar player who was so bad that even the lead singer noticed?!?!

Q: What do a vacuum cleaner and an electric guitar have in common?
A: Both suck when you plug them in.

Q: What is the traditional greeting between guitarists?
A: "Hi, I'm better than you!"

"To use a woman or a guitar, one must know how to tune them"
Spanish Proverb

"We don't like their sound, and guitar music is on the way out"
Decca Recording Executive
Upon rejecting The Beatles in January 1962

"If you think of four Brooke Bond chimps on very strong drugs, then that would be very close to how we were"

Gary 'Mani' Mountfield The Stone Roses

"We're not arrogant, we just think we're the best band in the world"

Noel Gallagher Oasis

"Has-beens shouldn't present awards to gonna-bes"

Noel Gallagher Oasis

After receiving the 1995 Brit Awards Best Album Award from ex-INXS frontman Michael Hutchence

"Rock journalism: people who can't write doing interviews with people who can't think in order to prepare articles for people who can't read"

Frank Zappa American Composer/
Rock Musician/Guitarist

Guitarist: Doctor, doctor – I've broken a string.
Doctor: You mustn't fret.

guitarist n. Someone who likes to get attention, but can't sing.

Guitars

"Knowledge speaks...but wisdom listens"

Jimi Hendrix American Rock Guitarist/Singer/Songwriter

Q: What did the guitarist do when his teacher told him to turn his amplifier on?
A: He caressed it softly and told it that he loved it.

"It's been through three wives. To me a guitar is kind of like a woman. You don't know why you like 'em but you do"

Waylon Jennings Country Singer/Guitarist
About his Telecaster guitar

Q: What do you throw a drowning lead guitarist?
A: His amp.

"Having played with other musicians, I don't even think The Beatles were that good"

George Harrison
Singer/Songwriter/Guitarist/Member of The Beatles

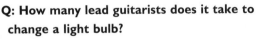

Q: How many lead guitarists does it take to change a light bulb?
A: None. They just steal someone else's light.

Banjos

What's the fastest way to tune a banjo?

Q: What's the fastest way to tune a banjo?
A: Wire cutters.

The banjo is right up there with the drum kit as the butt of musicians' derision. Seen as an unsophisticated instrument with a high annoyance factor, it acts as a lightning conductor for all those musical jokes you can transfer to whatever instrument you hate most...

Brett Butler, star of the U.S. sitcom Grace Under Fire and a stand-up comic from the American South, was reluctantly dragged along to the opera in New York by her music-loving husband. When the performance had finished he asked what she thought of it. "Not much," she said. "I expect you miss the banjos," he replied.

Banjos

People who never miss the banjos came up with these...

"Banjos are to music, what Spam is to food."

"Banjo tuning is an oxymoron."

"On a banjo, frets are like speed bumps."

Q: What's the difference between a banjo and a cattle grid?
A: People slow down before they drive over a cattle grid.

Q: How many banjo players does it take to change a light bulb?
A: Two. One to screw it in and one to complain that it's electric.

Q: What's the difference between a banjo player and a locksmith?

A: A locksmith gets paid to change keys.

Q: How many strings does a banjo have?

A: Five too many.

A Russian, a Cuban and two American musicians –
a guitarist and a banjo player – share a compartment
on a train. The Russian boasts that in his country they
have so much vodka they can afford to throw it away.
He demonstrates by throwing a bottle of premium
Russian vodka out of the window onto the track.
The Cuban, anxious not to be outdone, says,
"In Cuba we have so many fine cigars, they're worth
almost nothing". To demonstrate, he throws a box
of fine Havana cigars out of the train window.
The American guitarist says nothing. He just stands
up and throws the banjo player out of the window.

Q: How many banjo jokes are there?
A: Only three – the rest are true stories.

Banjos

A musician, who's also an animal lover, sees a giant
rat in a London shop window. He goes in and on a
whim buys it. He starts walking down the street
with his new pet and gradually starts to notice two or
three more giant rats following him. He walks a bit
faster but gradually more and more giant rats join
the procession. He starts running, but by the time he
gets to the Embankment every giant rat in London
seems to be following him. In a panic he throws his
rat into the river and, lo and behold, all the other rats
jump in after it. The musician stops, thinks a bit and
makes his way back to the shop where he bought it.
He goes up to the man who sold him the giant rat
and says, "You haven't got any giant banjos have you?"

**Q: What do you call a good musician at a
  banjo contest?**
  A: Lost.

Q: What's the easiest way for a banjo player to make money?
A: Threaten to play.

....

"There's nothing I like better
than the sound of a banjo, unless of
course it's the sound of a
chicken caught in a vacuum cleaner"
Anonymous

....

Q: How can you tell the difference between banjo tunes?

A: By the titles.

....

"I'd rather have a bottle in front of me than a frontal lobotomy"

Tom Waits American Songwriter/Composer/Pianist

Banjos

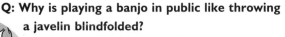

Q: Why is playing a banjo in public like throwing a javelin blindfolded?

A: You don't have to be very good at either to get people's attention.

Drummers & Percussionists

What do you call someone
who hangs around with musicians?

Q: What do you call someone who hangs around with musicians?
A: A drummer.

Timing Is Everything

There's a famous story about the jazz drummer who was doing a spell of playing in the pit for My Fair Lady. There was a very long break and he fell asleep. When he suddenly woke up, he was convinced that this was the point in the production when he was supposed to strike a gong – so he did. It was immediately clear from everybody's reaction that this was not the right moment for the gong. In the ensuing silence he stood up, turned to the audience and said, "Ladies and Gentlemen, dinner is served..."

....

"A lot of fellows nowadays have a B.A., M.D., or Ph.D. Unfortunately they don't have a J.O.B."

Fats Domino American Rock 'n' Roll Singer/ Pianist/Songwriter

....

Q: How do you make a drummer keep playing?
A: Glare at him and make frantic gestures indicating that he should stop.

In a music school the professor asked the drummer, "Can you please tell us the subdominant of F major?" After a few minutes of off-put silence, the drummer replied, "Hold on a minute, you can't fool me – F major is already the subdominant!"

Q: What did the percussionist have with his soup?
A: A drum roll.

Q: What's the difference between a drummer and a drum machine?
A: You only have to punch the information into the drum machine once.

81

Q: How do you get a drummer to stop playing?
A: Give him his cue.

Take Five

A trio was playing at a dance, when suddenly the piano player leant over to the bass player and said, "I've really got to go to the toilet. You just keep playing." The bass player said, "OK". The pianist then disappeared and the bass player and the drummer kept playing away. After 15 minutes there was no sign of the third member of the trio, so the bass player said to the drummer, "You keep playing and I'll go and look for him." The bass player found the piano player sitting in the bar. "So what are you doing?" he asked. "Oh, I'm fed up with this," replied the pianist, "I'm having a drink – why don't you have one too?" So now they were both sitting there drinking and the drummer was left to keep on playing alone. After 15 minutes of this, one of the dancers called out to the drummer, "Can you play The Lady Is A Tramp?", to which the drummer replied – "What do you think I'm playing?"

Q: What do you call a percussion instrument at an auction?

A: Going-going-gong.

....

"I hope the fans will take up meditation instead of drugs"

Ringo Starr The Beatles Drummer/Singer/Songwriter

....

Q: How do you get a drummer to play an accelerando?

A: You ask him to play 4/4 at a constant 120 beats per minute.

Q: Did you hear about the heavy metal player who locked his keys in the car?
A: He had to break the window to let the drummer out.

Q: How can you tell if the stage is level?
A: The drummer drools out of both sides of his mouth.

Q: What do you call a drummer who just broke up with his girlfriend?
A: Homeless.

....

"Some drummers think time is only a magazine"

Bobby Sanabria Jazz Drummer

....

Q: Why do drummers have half an ounce more brains than horses?
A: So they don't disgrace themselves during the parade.

Q: How many drummers does it take to change a light bulb?
A: None. They have machines to do that now.

....

"We never play anything the same way once"

Shelly Manne Jazz Drummer

....

Q: What did the drummer get on his I.Q. test?
A: Drool.

Drummers & Percussionists

Q: What do you call a drummer in a three-piece suit?
A: The defendant.

Q: What do you call a drummer with half a brain?
A: Gifted.

Q: Why do bands have a bass player?
A: To translate for the drummer.

Q: How do you know when a drummer is at your door?
A: The knock speeds up.

Said the bass player to the drummer, "Can't you play a little more dynamic?" Replied the drummer, "I'm already playing a loud as I can."

"I'm not going to say anything because nobody believes me when I do"

Ringo Starr The Beatles Drummer/Singer/Songwriter

Once upon a time, a drummer wanted to study music. During his entrance exam at the conservatory he was played a C and an E and asked to identify what he heard. His vexed expression indicated that he had no idea which interval it could possibly be. He asked, "Could I hear that again?... I'm not quite sure yet." Again he was played a C followed by an E. "Hmmm, I don't know... once again please, then I think I'll have it." So once more he was played a C and an E. Suddenly, his face lit up and he shouted, "I know! It's a piano, isn't it?"

Q: How can you tell that a drummer is walking behind you?
A: You can hear his knuckles dragging on the ground.

Q: What do you get when you cross a gamelan orchestra with Scarlett O'Hara?
A: Gong With The Wind.

Q: Why are concert intervals limited to 20 minutes?
A: So you don't have to retrain drummers.

A Big Break

There is a true story about the drummer in Ken Colyer's Trad Jazz band, whose bass pedal broke while they were touring Germany. This robbed the band of its overpowering bass rhythm, but they decided to soldier on without it. On the first night's gig, after the loss of the pedal, Colyer turned to his suddenly audible bass player and asked, "Have you always played like that?" The bass player replied, "Yes", and Colyer said, "Well, you're fired then."

Q: What did the marimba say to the xylophone?
A: "Who's got the vibe...?"

....

"In the orchestra, percussion instruments are effective in inverse proportion to their number"

Charles Villiers Stanford
British Composer/Conductor

....

Two cowboys were lost in North American Indian territory, sitting round the campfire. They were already nervous when suddenly the sound of war drums was heard from beyond the trees. One turned to the other and said, "Hank, I sure don't like the sound of them drums." And a voice came out from behind the trees... "He's not our regular drummer!"

Q: What's the best thing to play a bodhran with?
A: A razor blade.

Pianos

Why was the piano invented?

Q: Why was the piano invented?
A: So the musician would have a place to put his beer.

Pianos

Q: Why is an 11-foot concert grand better than
a studio upright?
A: Because it makes a much bigger ka-boom
when dropped over a cliff.

> ## "I know two kinds of audience only – one coughing and one not coughing"
> **Artur Schnabel** Austrian Pianist/Composer

Star Treatment

When Jim Reeves played in Ireland, he got to the venue and found he had been provided with a terrible hall and his accompanist had been given a dreadful old upright piano with half the notes missing. When Reeves gently pointed out that his contract stipulated a grand piano, the reply came, "Sir, I assure you this is the grandest piano in all Ireland."

> ## "You play Bach your way and I'll play him his way"
> **Wanda Landowska** Polish Keyboard Player/Composer

The audience at a piano recital were appalled when a telephone rang just offstage. Without missing a note, the soloist glanced toward the wings and called, "If that's my agent, tell him I'm working!"

Q: How many good accompanists can you fit in a phone booth?
A: Both of them.

Q: What's better than roses on top of the piano?
A: Tulips around your organ.

"Applause is a receipt, not a note of demand"

Artur Schnabel Austrian Pianist/Composer

"Old piano players never die, they simply fake away"

Anonymous

piano n. A parlour utensil for subduing the impenitent visitor. It is operated by depressing the keys of the machine and the spirits of the audience.

Ambrose Bierce The Devil's Dictionary, 1911

Pianos

"A piano is a lot more useful than a synthesizer. You can make a synthesizer sound like a piano, you can get a sample which produces an exact replica of the noise. But you can't stand on a synthesizer, you can't jump up and down on a synthesizer, you can't do a back-flip off a synthesizer. A piano comes in handy for that kind of stuff."

Billy Joel Rock Singer/Songwriter/Pianist

"Over the piano was printed a notice: 'Please do not shoot the pianist. He is doing his best'"

Oscar Wilde Irish Playwright

Conductors

What's the difference between a conductor and a sack of manure?

Q: **What's the difference between a conductor and a sack of manure?**
A: The sack.

Q: **Why are conductors' hearts much sought after for transplants?**
A: Because they have had very little use.

A blind rabbit and a blind snake bumped into each other in the forest. The rabbit said, "Watch where you are going! Can't you see that I am blind?" The snake replied, "No. I can't see that you are blind, because I am blind myself."
Then the rabbit had a brilliant idea. "Why don't we feel each other and guess what the other is?" The snake accepted this proposal and went first. The snake said, "Let's see – you're furry with long ears and a cotton tail...you must be a rabbit." "Very good," said the rabbit, "Now it's my turn. You are cold, slimy, spineless and have no ears...you must be a conductor."

Q: **How are conductors and condoms similar?**
A: It's safer with them, but more fun without.

....

"In music one must think with the heart and feel with the brain"

George Szell American Conductor

....

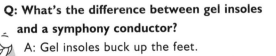

Q: **What's the difference between gel insoles and a symphony conductor?**
A: Gel insoles buck up the feet.

Q: What's the difference between God and a conductor?

A: God knows he's not a conductor.

Q: What's the difference between a bull and an orchestra?

A: The bull has the horns at the front and the asshole at the back.

Q: What's the definition of an assistant conductor?
A: A mouse trying to become a rat.

An American orchestra had just arrived in
Europe for a two-week tour. One hour before the
first concert, the conductor became ill and was
unable to conduct – the orchestra suddenly had
to find a substitute.

The orchestral manager asked the orchestra whether
anyone could step in and conduct, and the only person
who was willing was the last chair violist.

The manager was very nervous about this.

"We can't audition you..." he said.

"No problem," replied the violist.

"There's no time to rehearse – you'll have to do the
concert cold..."

"I know. It'll be alright."

The violist conducted the concert and it was a
smashing success. Since the conductor remained ill
for the duration of the tour, the violist conducted
all of the concerts, getting rave reviews and standing
ovations at every one.

At the next rehearsal, the conductor had recovered,
and the violist returned to his place at the back of the
viola section. As he sat down, his desk partner asked
him, "Where've you been for the last two weeks?"

**Q: Did you hear about the planeload of conductors
en route to a European music festival?**
A: The good news is it crashed – the bad news is that
there were three empty seats on board.

Q: What's the ideal weight of a conductor?
A: 28 ounces, including the urn.

Q: What's the difference between a pig and a symphony conductor?
A: There are some things a pig just isn't willing to do.

Q: What's the difference between an opera conductor and a baby?
A: A baby sucks its fingers.

A musician called the symphony office to talk to the conductor. "I'm sorry, he's dead," came the reply. The musician called back 25 times, always getting the same reply from the receptionist. At last she asked him why he kept calling. "I just like to hear you say it."

After a succession of effusive tributes, telegrams and letters from composers, conductors and musicians congratulating him on his seventieth birthday, Sir Thomas Beecham asked innocently, "What! Nothing from Mozart?"

conductor n. A musician who is adept at following many people at the same time.

In the beginning, there were only wind instruments in the orchestra. Then they noticed that many of the people were too stupid to play wind instruments, so they gave them large boxes with wires strapped across them. These people were known as 'string players'. Then they realised that some people were too dumb to play string instruments, so they were given two sticks and were told to hit whatever they wanted. These people were known as 'percussionists'. Finally, they spotted that one percussionist was so dumb, he couldn't even do that, so they took away one of his sticks and told him to go and stand in front of everybody – and that was the birth of the 'conductor'.

Conductors

....

"James Agate, meeting a friend, a member of the BBC orchestra: 'Who conducted this afternoon?' Alec Whittaker, First Oboe: 'Sorry James, I forgot to look'"

Jacques Barzun American Historian/Critic

....

Composers

What's the most painful dance in Russia?

Q: What's the most painful dance in Russia?
A: Tchaikovsky's *Nutcracker*.

Q: What did the harpsichord repairman say to Bach?
A: If it ain't Baroque, don't fix it.

Q: What do you get when Mike Oldfield farts on the underground?
A: Tubular Smells.

> "We're not interested in writing for posterity. We just want it to sound good right now!"
>
> **Duke Ellington** American Jazz Composer/
> Bandleader/Pianist

> "Syncopation is in the soul of every true American"
>
> **Irving Berlin** American Composer/Songwriter

> "Jazz is the result of the energy stored up in America"
>
> **George Gershwin** American Composer/Songwriter

Q: Why was Satie standing at the side of the road?
A: He was waiting for Debussy.

> "Creative people have to be fed from the divine source. We have to get fed. We have to get filled up in order to pour out"
>
> **Johnny Cash** Country Singer/Songwriter

A note left for a composer from his wife:

Gone Chopin, (have Liszt), Bach in a Minuet

> "Composing is not a profession.
> It is a mania – a harmless madness"
>
> **Arthur Honegger** Swiss-French Composer

> "I don't like composers who think.
> It gets in the way of their plagiarism"
>
> **Howard Dietz** American Lyricist

Q: Why did Tchaikovsky move around all the time?
A: Because he composed a piece in five flats.

Composers

> "I don't like my music but
> what is my opinion against that of
> millions of others?"
>
> **Frederick Loewe** American Composer of Musicals

> "All the inspiration I ever needed
> was a phonecall from a producer"
>
> **Cole Porter** American Composer/Songwriter

> "Handel is only fourth rate.
> He is not even interesting"
>
> **Pyotr Tchaikovsky** Russian Composer

Q: Why couldn't Mozart find a friend?
A: Because he was Haydn.

"A good composer does not imitate, he steals"

Igor Stravinsky Russian Composer

Q: We know that Bach had bad eyesight, but what about his teeth?

A: They weren't much better – too many suites.

"Before I compose a piece
I walk round it several times,
accompanied by myself"

Erik Satie French Composer

"It is sobering to consider that
when Mozart was my age he had
already been dead for a year"

Tom Lehrer American Composer of Satirical Songs

"The public doesn't want new music;
the main thing that it demands
of a composer is that he be dead"

Arthur Honegger Swiss-French Composer

"A film musician is like a
mortician – he can't bring the body
back to life, but he's
expected to make it look better"

Adolph Deutsch Film Composer

"Wagner has lovely moments
but awful quarters of an hour"

Gioachino Rossini Italian Composer

Patient: Doctor, Doctor, I can't stop singing
the Hallelujah Chorus!
Doctor: Well, get a Handel on yourself man!

Composers

Singers

What was inscribed on
the tombstone of a Blues singer?

Q: What was inscribed on the tombstone of a Blues
singer?
A: Didn't wake up this morning...

....

"In opera there is always too much singing"

Claude Debussy French Composer

....

"Opera – the most rococo and degraded of all forms of art"

William Morris British Craftsman/Designer/Writer/
Typographer/Socialist

Singers

transposition *n. The act of moving the relative pitch of a
piece of music that is too low for the basses to a point at which
it is too high for the sopranos.*

Q: What do you call a soprano who can sight-read?
A: An alto.

Q: What do 10 opera singers in a small transit sing?
A: Cosy Van Tutti.

....

"No good opera plot can be sensible, for people do not sing when they are feeling sensible"

W H Auden English Poet

....

Q: What do you call a singer who keeps repeating herself?

A: Lesley Parrot.

Q: At which concert venue will you always get bad reviews?

A: The Royal Flopera House.

Q: What's the difference between a Wagnerian soprano and a Wagnerian tenor?

A: About 10 pounds.

Q: If you threw a violist and a soprano off a cliff, which one would hit the ground first?

A: The violist. The soprano would have to stop halfway down to ask directions.

vibrato n. A technique used by singers to hide the fact that they are on the wrong pitch.

"I sometimes wonder which would be nicer – an opera without an interval, or an interval without an opera"

Ernest Newman English Writer on Music

"There was a time when I heard eleven operas in a fortnight... which left me bankrupt and half idiotic for a month"

JB Priestley British Author/Novelist/Playwright

"The high note is not the only thing"

Placido Domingo Opera Singer

Q: What's the first thing a soprano does in the morning?

A: Gets up and goes home.

"Grand opera will never pay"

Sir Thomas Beecham English Conductor

"We cannot direct the wind, but we can adjust the sails"

Dolly Parton American Singer

"I don't mean to be a diva, but some days you wake up and you're Barbara Streisand"

Courtney Love American Singer

"The first act [of Parsifal] occupied two hours, and I enjoyed that in spite of the singing"

Mark Twain American Writer

After interrupting a rehearsal several times while a soprano soloist went astray, conductor Sir Thomas Beecham asked in exasperation, "Madam, have you looked at this score before?" "Indeed, Sir Thomas," came the indignant reply. "I have eaten, drunk and slept with Messiah for weeks!"

"Then of course you must have an immaculate conception of the role."

Q: What's the difference between a soprano and a piranha?

A: The lipstick.

Singers

"Sleep is an excellent way of listening to an opera"

James Stephens Irish Poet/Fiction Writer

....

"My voice is small but disagreeable"

George Gershwin American Composer/Songwriter

....

Q: How many Country & Western singers does it take to change a light bulb?

A: Three. One to change the bulb and two to sing about the old one.

"Convicts are the best audiences I ever played for"

Johnny Cash Country Singer/Songwriter

"I haven't heard anything like that since the orphanage burned down"

Mark Twain American Writer

When asked what he thought of an opera he had just attended

coloratura soprano n. A singer who has great trouble finding the proper note, but has a wild time hunting for it.

Q: How do you tell if a tenor is dead?
A: The wine bottle is still full and the comics haven't been touched.

"I like most of the places I've been to, but I've never really wanted to go to Japan, simply because I don't really like eating fish, and I know that's very popular out there in Africa"

Britney Spears American Pop Singer

"I never knew how good our songs were until I heard Ella Fitzgerald sing them"

Ira Gershwin American Lyricist

Q: What's the difference between a soprano and a pit bull?

A: The jewellery.

....

"A tenor is not a man but a disease"

Hans von Bülow German Pianist/Conductor

....

"Now, ladies and contraltos, if you will look to your parts, you'll see where the gentlemen and the tenors come in"

Sir Thomas Beecham Conductor

preparatory beat *n. A threat made to singers, i.e. sing, or else...*

Singers

"The opera house is an institution differing from other lunatic asylums only in the fact that its inmates have avoided official certification"

Ernest Newman English Writer on Music

....

"How wonderful opera would be if there were no singers"

Gioachino Rossini Italian Composer

....

Q: What's the definition of a male quartet?

A: Three men and a tenor.

Accordions

What is an accordion good for?

Q: What is an accordion good for?
A: To learn how to fold a map.

The definition of a true lady or gentleman, is someone who can play the accordion...but doesn't.

accordion n. *An instrument in harmony with the sentiments of an assassin.*
Ambrose Bierce *The Devil's Dictionary, 1911*

Accordions

Two people, just entering the afterlife, get a slightly different treatment...

"Welcome to Heaven, here's your harp!"

"Welcome to Hell, here's your accordion!"

The Best of the Rest...

What do you do when a working musician
comes to your front door?

Q: What do you do when a working musician comes to your front door?
A: You give him the money and take the pizza.

Q: What does an Irishman call a good bowel movement?
A: A major turd.

....

"I want to keep making records as long as I can, but I don't know how long you can be taken seriously in rap"

Eminen Rapper

....

"I don't know anything about music. In my line you don't have to"

Elvis Presley

....

Q: What do you get after you've run over an army officer with a steam roller?
A: A flat major.

....

"Some people tap their feet, some people snap their fingers, and some people sway back and forth. I just sorta do 'em all together, I guess"

Elvis Presley

Talking about his way of moving on stage

....

Q: What do fish play?
A: Scales.

....

"I'm an ocean, because I'm
really deep. If you search deep enough
you can find rare exotic treasures"

Christina Aguilera Pop Singer

....

Q: What key is *Exploring Caves With No Flashlight*
written in?
A: See sharp or be flat.

Q: What happens when you play a blues record backwards?

A: You are released from prison, your wife returns to you and your dog comes back to life.

Q: What do you get when an army officer puts his nose to the grindstone?

A: A sharp major.

"Today you play jazz, tomorrow you will betray your country"
Stalinist Era Poster

"I get to go to lots of overseas places, like Canada"
Britney Spears American Pop Singer

ad libitum *adj.* A premiere.

Q: How many producers does it take to change a light bulb?

A: Hmmm...I don't know...What do you think?

Q: What happens when you see Cat Stevens naked in the twilight?

A: You get a *Moonshadow*.

Q: Where does Kylie buy her kebabs from?

A: Jason's Doner Van.

Q: What do you call a small fella who rides the tube?
A: A Metro-gnome.

Q: Which band needs ironing out?
A: The Kinks.

"By definition pop is extremely catchy, whether you like it or not. There are some pop songs I hate but I can't get them out of my head. Our songs also have the standard pop format: Verse, chorus, verse, chorus, solo, bad solo. All in all, I think we sound like The Knack and the Bay City Rollers being molested by Black Flag and Black Sabbath"

Kurt Cobain Lead Singer & Guitarist in Nirvana

"I found my inner bitch and ran with her"

Courtney Love American Singer

"Never met a wise man. If so, it's a woman!"

Kurt Cobain Lead Singer & Guitarist in Nirvana

Q: Where do you put noisy babies?
A: In a crèche-endo.

Q: Who was Shakespeare's favourite band?

A: Sonnet & Cher.

Q: Who's the sweetest of all 80s pop stars?

A: Simon Le Bon-Bon.

> "Reggae music is one of them stones that was refused by the builders"
>
> **Charlie Ace** Reggae Musician

Q: Why do bagpipe players march when they play?
A: To get away from the sound.

> "Punk is musical freedom. It's saying, doing and playing what you want. In Webster's terms, 'nirvana' means freedom from pain, suffering and the external world, and that's pretty close to my definition of Punk Rock"
>
> **Kurt Cobain** Lead Singer & Guitarist in Nirvana

> "Country music is three chords and the truth"
>
> **Harlan Howard** Country Singer/Songwriter

Q: Who cuts Jim'll Fix It's hair?
A: The Barber of Saville.

Q: What do you get if you combine diminished and augmented chords?
A: Demented chords.

Saint Peter was checking IDs at the Pearly Gates, when along came a Texan.

"Tell me, what did you do in life?" asked St Peter. The Texan replied, "Well, I struck oil, I became rich, but I didn't sit on my laurels – I divided all my money among my entire family in my will, so our descendants are all set for about three generations."

St Peter said, "That's quite something. Come on in. Next!"

The next guy in line had been listening, so he said, "I struck it big in the stock market, but I didn't selfishly just provide for my own like that Texan guy. I donated five million to Save the Children."

"Wonderful!" said St Peter, "Come in. Who's next?"

The third guy had also been listening and said timidly with a downcast look, "Well, I only made five thousand pounds in my entire lifetime."

"Heavens!" said St Peter, "And what instrument did you play?"

....

"All I know is what I read in the papers. I don't care, so long as they don't drop the bomb before I get a chance to make money"

Jimi Hendrix On politics

....

Q: How many punk rockers does it take to change a light bulb?

A: Two. One who screws and one who smashes the old one on his forehead.

Q: What do you call three hairy rockers drinking lemonade?
A: ZZ-Pop.

Q: What do Indie rockers have on their stairs?
A: Inspiral Carpets.

Q: What do you call a teeny-weeny crisp?
A: A hemidemisemiquaver.

Q: What do you get when you drop a piano down a mine shaft?

A: A flat minor.

Q: What do you call a whistling hat?

A: A trill-by.

"I was a veteran before I was a teenager"

Michael Jackson Pop Singer/Songwriter/Producer

"I performed at Mom and Dad's party when I was four.
Oh my gosh, I was singing a Madonna song and I peed myself"

Britney Spears Pop Singer

"Maybe I'll go to college someday, for that knowledge, but I definitely think making music always will be the most important thing in my life"

Britney Spears Pop Singer

"I'm just like anyone. I cut and I bleed. And I embarrass easily"

Michael Jackson Pop Singer/Songwriter/Producer

Q: **What did the bouncer say when Queen tried to get into a nightclub?**
A: Freddie, Roger & John can't come in – but Brian May.

Q: **How many stage hands does it take to change a light bulb?**
A: One, two...one, two...

"We pity anybody who doesn't buy our records"

Liam Gallagher Oasis

Q: What happens if you haven't got anyone to play with?
A: You'll have to duet yourself.

The Best of the Rest...

"It [LSD] opened my eyes. We only use one-tenth of our brain. Just think of what we could accomplish if we could only tap that hidden part! It would mean a whole new world if the politicians would take LSD. There wouldn't be any more war or poverty or famine"

Paul McCartney Pop Singer/Songwriter/
Instrumentalist/Composer/Member of The Beatles

"Me and Janet really are two different people"

Michael Jackson Pop Singer/Songwriter/Producer

Q: What do you get when you play New Age music backwards?
A: New Age music.

..and especially Folk Music
What's 30 feet wide and has eight teeth?

Q: What's 30 feet wide and has eight teeth?
A: The front row at the Grand Ole Opry.

126

...and especially Folk Music

Q: What is the professional folk musician's ultimate sexual fantasy?
A: A girlfriend with a job.

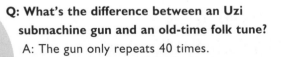

Q: What's the difference between an Uzi submachine gun and an old-time folk tune?
A: The gun only repeats 40 times.

"All music is folk music. I ain't never heard no horse sing a song"

Louis Armstrong American Jazz Trumpeter/
Singer/Bandleader

Q: What's the difference between folk and bluegrass?
A: If you practice, tune your instrument and make a sound check before you start playing, it's folk. Otherwise, it's bluegrass.

Q: What's the difference between an insurance policy and a folk musician?
A: The insurance policy will eventually mature and earn money.

"You can't write a good song about a whorehouse unless you been in one"

Woody Guthrie American Folksinger/Songwriter

Q: How many traditional folk musicians does it take to change a light bulb?
A: Six. One to change the bulb, and five to complain that it's electric and bitch about how much mellower a candle would be.

folk singer *n. Someone who sings through his nose what he heard through his ears.*